CW00972804

*The ancient monuments of*
# Shetland

Text by Noel Fojut and Denys Pringle
Edited by Chris Tabraham
Designed by Derek Munn  HMSO Graphic Design Edinburgh
Principal photography David Henrie
Additional photography by Mike Brooks, Noel Fojut and Denys Pringle

*1*

1. Stanydale
2. Clickhimin
3. Ness of Burgi
4. Mousa Broch
5. Jarlshof
6. Muness Castle
7. Scalloway Castle
8. Fort Charlotte

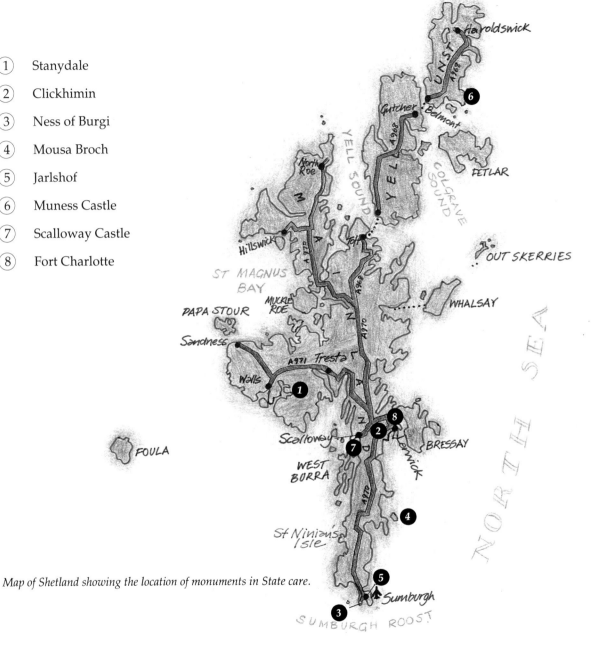

*Map of Shetland showing the location of monuments in State care.*

*Typical Shetland coastline: Kame of Isbister.*

Shetland is an archipelago of over one hundred islands, less than twenty of which are now inhabited. It occupies a maritime crossroads where the North Sea meets the Atlantic Ocean, almost equidistant from Aberdeen in Scotland, Bergen in Norway and Torshavn in Faroe. Regarded for much of its past as being at the end of the world - it was almost certainly the Ultima Thule of Roman writers - it has formed at other times a stepping stone for movements of people, goods and ideas.

The islands that comprise Shetland are the top of a drowned range of hills. The rocks are old and hard, and although the colourful glitter of granite and gneiss to be seen in a structure such as **Muness Castle** is attractive, the labour involved in shaping building blocks from such intractable materials was considerable. Only in the extreme south and east of the islands is good building stone available - grey-brown flagstones which give a distinctive appearance to the buildings of Lerwick and the south. Around the edges of the islands are steep cliffs, but long inlets or voes lead between these into a gentler landscape of low shingly shores and long, whale-backed hills.

Shetland's climate is oceanic - mild in winter and cool in summer. Rainfall is not particularly high, but is distributed evenly throughout the year, so the islands seldom experience drought. The dominant feature is the wind, with gales frequent. Windforce and saltspray combine to reduce vegetation to a low and stunted state, and trees are rare.

*Unpromising material: some of Shetland's best building stone.*

Shetland's windswept shores have provided a livelihood for hardy farmers and fishermen for at least five-and-a-half thousand years. The islands boast some of the most complete Neolithic and Bronze-Age farming landscapes anywhere in Europe, though much of this evidence is not striking to the eye. The succeeding Iron Age provides a contrast, with the most complete Iron-Age fortification in Scotland, **Mousa Broch**, and a series of other fortified sites.

Shetland was settled early in the Viking colonisation of the Atlantic islands and became for centuries a centre of communication for the Norse world. Even after their transfer to Scotland in 1469, the islands were frequently of strategic importance. This, combined with the seafaring skills of Shetlanders, meant that the islands were always surprisingly cosmopolitan in outlook, and this is reflected in the range of modest but accomplished medieval and more recent buildings: churches, castles and houses.

Some of the most important ancient monuments in Shetland are cared for by HISTORIC SCOTLAND on behalf of the Secretary of State for Scotland. These eight sites, shown in **bold** type in this book, are readily accessible to visitors. Reference to any other site does not imply public access. The eight sites together cover the whole spectrum of human habitation in Shetland, from the Neolithic complex at **Stanydale** to the eighteenth-century **Fort Charlotte** in Lerwick. This book places each site in its historical context and guides the visitor around the surviving remains. The extraordinary archaeological site at **Jarlshof**, which was continuously inhabited almost from the beginning of human settlement in Shetland until its abandonment in the seventeenth century, has its own guidebook, but frequent reference is made to it in this book to furnish important details absent from the other monuments and, in particular, to provide an insight into the Norse settlement.

*Mousa Broch*, almost perfect after 2000 years.

The first Shetlanders were Neolithic farmers who had reached the islands by 3600 BC. At about that date several individuals were laid to rest in a large stone cist at Sumburgh, near to **Jarlshof**. These people, or their recent ancestors, had most likely come from Orkney, probably after sending out scouts to explore and assess the prospects for permanent settlement. Fair Isle and Foula in Shetland would have been just visible to them on a clear day from the top of Westray and North Ronaldsay in Orkney, as they are today.

At the time of its first settlement, and for centuries thereafter, Shetland had a kinder climate, with higher average temperatures and less wind. Sea-level was considerably lower, so there was more fertile ground around the shores than now. On landing from their skin-covered boats the newcomers would have found a landscape of gentle hills covered by low, scrubby forest of alder, willow, hazel and birch. Small copses of taller trees would have occupied sheltered locations. Apart from seals and otters there were no land mammals. These settlers, however, arrived with cattle and sheep, and probably dogs to help herd them. Pigs and hens may have been introduced much later.

The grazing of animals and the clearance of woodland to create arable land for growing barley gradually led to the creation of a more open landscape. The earliest dwellings may have been of wood, but soon, when all the larger trees had been cut and used for construction, stone became the normal building material for houses, with lesser buildings constructed in a mix of stone and turf. Enough woodland survived to supply lighter timber for framing roofs, thatched with heather and turf. This practice of building in stone and the lack of later intensive use of upland areas have resulted in the survival of a uniquely detailed Neolithic farming landscape, with the remains of houses, fields and piles of cleared stones scattered across the hill slopes.

*Shetland once looked like this, before the advent of man, grazing animals and climatic change.*

The dead were at first buried simply in stone-lined communal graves, but soon the construction of more elaborate chambered tombs began. These were also communal, but unlike the magnificent tombs of Orkney, those of Shetland are comparatively small, with modest chambers which could have accommodated only a handful of burials. Shetland tombs have a characteristic circular plan with a concave façade containing the entrance. For this reason they are usually referred to as "heel-shaped". Unfortunately, no tomb has been discovered in an undisturbed state; little can therefore be said about how the bodies were laid inside, or what artefacts were buried with the dead.

*Otter*

*Ward of Vementry chambered cairn.*

The approach on foot from the public road to the remarkable central structure at **Stanydale** passes through a typical area of prehistoric landscape, preserved by the later growth of peat from 2000 BC onwards, which turned marginal farmland into intractable moor.

*U 285502*
*oadside parking;*
*3 mile moorland*
*alk to monument.*

The route climbs over a low ridge and into a broad basin. Several of the hills that rim this basin are topped by the ruins of burial cairns. As the path crosses this low basin, a tumbled mass of grey stone may be seen to the left, beside a marker pole. This represents the remains of a simple oval farmhouse, which was excavated in the 1950s. Its entrance is at the far end, flanked by a windbreak wall, and a small chamber is set in the thickness of the wall at the inner end, perhaps representing a bed-recess.

Such houses are widespread in Shetland. Indeed, so common are they that, when they were first noted, archaeologists refused to believe that they could be of any great age. They are now known to have been built from at least 3000 BC to 500 BC, and perhaps later. Usually they consist of a large main room, oval in plan, with two or four bed-recesses on either side of a central hearth, in which a peat fire burned. The walls were probably low, perhaps topped with turf, and the roof was of light timber covered with turf-and-heather thatch. Smoke issued (if at all) from the low doorway, which provided the only daylight. During the long winter nights, lamps burning seal or seabird oil would have given a dim light within. Prehistoric Shetlanders, like their later counterparts, probably spent much of their day out of doors, on the farm, on the shore or at sea.

Beyond the house, a scatter of low mounds may be seen emerging from the peaty soil. These represent cairns of stones gathered in antiquity from fields now long-abandoned. Stretches of tumbled walling can be seen running off up the hillsides. Since the Neolithic farmers used quite fragile ploughs of wood with stone tips, it was necessary to remove all large stones from the soil: these were used to make walls and, when all the walls were built, the rest were simply piled up in unused corners to form "clearance cairns".

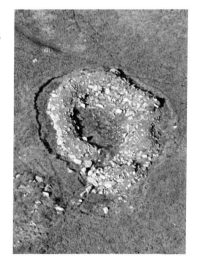

**Stanydale:** *foundations of a Neolithic house.*

**Stanydale**: *the "temple" interior.*

At the inner end of the valley, flanked by a curving line of standing stones, are the remains of the impressive structure called the " Stanydale temple". This is the only truly megalithic (or "large-stone") structure to have survived from prehistoric Shetland, which lacks any great stone circles and tombs such as are found elsewhere in Scotland.

*The **Stanydale** "temple" reconstructed.*

The "temple" is in essence a double-sized version of the common prehistoric house, built probably between 2500 and 2000 BC. A wall of large boulders, 3-4 m thick, encloses an oval area 14 m by 10 m. Two large holes in the centre of this area held stout uprights of driftwood, including a species of pine from North America, which would have supported a roof. The construction of this would have been quite a feat around 2500 BC, when most of the native woodland in Shetland had already been cleared. Around the inner face of the walls of this building are recesses, similar to those interpreted as bed-recesses in normal prehistoric houses, but here again over-sized. There was no central hearth, but instead several small hearths lay near to the side walls, just outside the recesses. The entrance passage opens on the outside into a concave façade, which is very reminiscent of those of the Shetland heel-shaped burial cairns.

What was this structure? Was it, as the excavator suggested, a temple like those found in late Neolithic and Bronze-Age Malta? Certainly it resembles these in plan, but for anyone who has visited both islands the resemblance fails to convince. It seems too large to be just an ordinary house, even of a wealthy or powerful family. On excavation the interior was found to have been kept clean, while floors of ordinary houses are usually found to be covered by deep layers of ash, broken pottery and other domestic rubbish. The layout of the small hearths might suggest communal use - perhaps one family to each recess - but for what purpose? The building's construction would have entailed scouring the beaches for driftwood to roof it, and a communal effort in gathering and placing the great boulders incorporated in the walls. The façade suggests a link with whatever ritual practices were associated with the burial cairns.

Perhaps **Stanydale** was a temple, perhaps a village hall, a meeting-house, or a courtroom. Perhaps it was all or none of these things. We may never know, but **Stanydale** remains remarkable in a landscape characterised by an abundance of ordinary structures: simple houses, burial cairns and farms. And was this structure deliberately built in one of the very few places in Shetland from which the sea is invisible?

# Bronze-Age Shetland: a long decline

**S**tanydale "temple" was probably built between 2500 and 2000 BC. It was derelict by 1600 BC, for high in its ruins lay pottery sherds of a type associated with the early Bronze Age, a period which is thought to have begun about 1800 BC; at that time worked metal began to supplement stone, wood and bone as a raw material for tool-making, though bronze was probably fairly scarce in Shetland throughout this period. Several of the ordinary prehistoric houses were also abandoned at about the same date. Why, if they once supported Neolithic farmers, are the upland slopes of Shetland now so singularly barren and devoid of human habitation?

From about 2000 BC, throughout north-west Europe, summers grew cooler and damper, and wind strengths increased. Crops grew less well, often failing to ripen. Shetland, just within the margins of feasibility for arable farming, was hard hit, and on the upper slopes it became impossible to grow barley. As the higher fields were abandoned to grazing, they began to accumulate a blanket of peat: dead vegetation, mostly moss, which could not rot down because of the cool, damp, conditions. On this peat, because of its acidity, only poor grass, heather or moss would grow. Poor farming practices, with bad drainage, over-cropping and removal of stones, may have helped encourage the spread of peat. This was an ecological disaster for the early Bronze-Age Shetlanders, but a great boon for later archaeologists, as the peat sealed beneath it the complete upland farming landscape as it was abandoned. Only with recent stripping of peat for fuel have these ancient remains come to light once again.

With the higher land rendered almost useless, people would have moved towards the shore, concentrating on land still low and fertile enough to grow grain. At this time, too, there was almost certainly an expansion in the use of marine resources, for the waters around Shetland were rich in fish and shellfish. Farming moved from a mixed, but predominantly arable, basis to a largely pastoral one. Remaining woodland was cleared for fuel and to create more farmland, and farmers who had once lived in scattered farmsteads found themselves gathered together into small townships, such as that represented by the cluster of houses at **Jarlshof**. Emigration was impossible: the rest of Europe to the south was also feeling the bite of this decline, while to the north-west the Faroes and Iceland were invisible and apparently unknown.

*A Bronze-Age house preserved among later remains at **Clickhimin**.*

At first, these changes seem to have led to communal co-operation rather than conflict. The activities required to supplement the impoverished farming economy, such as fishing or sea-bird and egg collecting, required group effort.

Another indication of communal activity is given by the curious "burnt mounds" frequently found beside streams. Burnt mounds are simply heaps of burnt stones, piled up in places where water was boiled in large wood- or stone-lined troughs by heating stones and throwing them in. The simplest explanation for them is that the boiling water was used for cooking large joints of meat, and perhaps "economical" foods such as puddings made of blood, meal and offal. Communal cooking in a fuel-efficient manner would certainly accord well with what we know of the straitened economic circumstances of the period, but more extravagant suggestions have also been advanced, such as their interpretation as sauna-baths or communal laundries. In Shetland they seem to be of Bronze-Age date (1800 to 600 BC), though elsewhere other dates have been recorded.

Oddly, in view of this communal activity in everyday matters, in the Bronze Age communal burial seems to have ceased, to be replaced by individual burial, under a small unchambered cairn, in a stone cist or directly into the ground. Possibly the harder living conditions did not allow enough spare time or surplus labour for the construction of elaborate cairns, and memorials may have taken simpler, less permanent forms.

*A burnt mound near Hillswick.*

*A prehistoric standing stone at Troswick ("Troll's Bay").*

Many of the standing stones scattered throughout Shetland may also have been erected in the Bronze Age. Their purpose is unknown, but they may have been associated with some long-forgotten ritual. There are no large stone circles in Shetland: indeed, except for the two splendid examples at **Brodgar** and **Stenness** in Orkney, large circles are not known in the north of Scotland.

By the end of the Bronze Age, Shetland was largely peat-covered and devoid of trees. Farming was restricted to a narrow coastal strip. Much of the farm work was probably done by women and children while the men fished, hunted seals and small whales, gathered eggs and climbed the cliffs for the plump young fledglings of puffin, razorbill, guillemot and even great auk - a choice delicacy whose bones have been found in Bronze-Age layers at **Jarlshof**. Diet was precarious but varied, and a highly organised social structure must have been needed to prevent disputes over scarce resources boiling over into conflict.

Very few houses from the later Bronze Age have been excavated. At **Jarlshof** houses seem to become progressively poorer throughout this period, while at **Clickhimin** a very small house seems to have served as the residence of a farming family shortly after 1000 BC.

*Now extinct, but once an important food source: the Great Auk.*

Eventually the apparently peaceful lifestyle of Bronze-Age Shetland proved inadequate, and in the succeeding Iron Age (600 BC - AD 500) defensive structures were built, indicating that some, or all, of those resident in Shetland feared attack.

Small-scale defences proliferated. Most were of the type called brochs, circular drystone towers. Ruins of 70 are known, and perhaps as many again once existed and have been totally lost. The broch of **Mousa**, described below, is the best preserved of these uniquely Scottish fortifications. In addition, Shetland has several simpler circular forts, or duns, and a variety of promontory forts with defences consisting of earthen banks, ditches and, in some cases, stone walls or elaborate masonry "blockhouses". Whether the builders were invaders, or, as seems more likely, the native inhabitants themselves, the construction of defences was probably organised by leaders, in a society which had by now developed a hierarchical form. The brochs, in particular, probably combined the role of a high-status dwelling for one family with that of an occasional refuge for a whole small community.

But against whom were these defences built? They could not have been for a lengthy defence, since there is little room for gathering food or property, though cattle (which would have been an important food resource, besides being used as a means of exchange ) might have been protected within the enclosures sometimes found attached to brochs. Few have a good long-term internal water-supply. So those who built them seem to have feared a short, sharp raid

Mousa Broch.

**Mousa Broch**: *remains of later modifications inside the broch.*

*A small fort on a loch-island in Burga Water, Sandness.*

aimed at inflicting death or capture. Although it has been suggested that the areas where brochs were built suffered from slave-raiding on a commercial scale, it seems most likely that the enemies against whom these forts were built were local: some neighbouring family with a grievance inflamed by bickering over rights to pasture or driftwood, or over cattle that had strayed, with or without help, on to another's land.

A need to provide secure storage for food led to the construction of underground stores below or beside houses. These stores took the form of small chambers reached by a passage covered by stone slabs. When rediscovered in more recent years they have been called souterrains, earth-houses or "pecht's hooses". Two fine examples may be seen at **Jarlshof**.

O n a low knoll beside the Loch of Clickhimin, near Lerwick, excavations have revealed a
remarkable sequence of structures which show how the needs of life changed from the
late Bronze Age into, and through, the Iron Age. The visible structures are complex,
and cannot easily be inspected in chronological sequence. They are described below in order of
construction, while the plan shows the best route around the site.

465408
*de South Road*
*ing Lerwick.*

1. Bronze-Age farmhouse

2. Ring wall

3. Blockhouse

4. Broch

5. Causeway

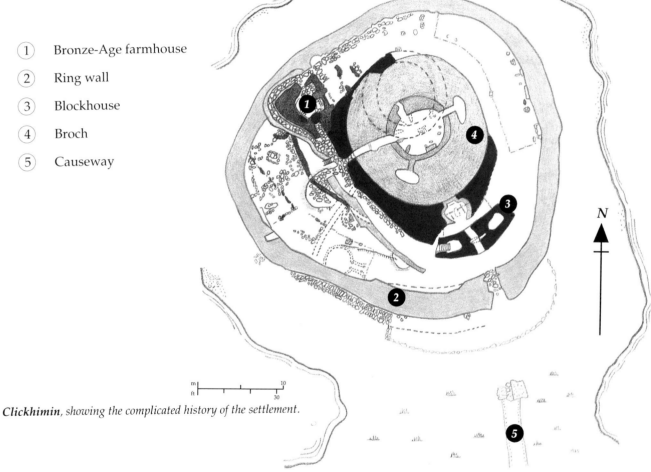

*Clickhimin, showing the complicated history of the settlement.*

A small late Bronze-Age farmhouse, with two side-chambers, and an attached outbuilding, were built at **Clickhimin** some time after 1000 BC (see page 13). They stood on a grassy knoll surrounded by a shallow loch or marshland, and the dry top of the knoll was walled to provide an enclosure for livestock. Barley was grown, and was ground into meal in large stone trough-querns (one of which may be seen on site). Local slate was used to fashion crude stone tools, but finer, highly polished stone knives were also used. These came from an area in the North Mainland of Shetland, and seem to be unique to the islands. Peat was doubtless used as fuel. At this date, as later, the main farmland and grazing would have been on the shores of the loch. This simple farmstead was still occupied when the first knowledge of the use of iron reached Shetland about 600 BC.

At a date between 300 and 100 BC the knoll was fortified. A stout masonry-faced wall was built, encircling the dry area, and a shallow ditch was dug across the isthmus that gave access to the site. This was probably crossed by a bridge, or drawbridge. The new ring-wall was entered through a narrow passageway, and lean-to wooden buildings were thrown up around its inner wall-face. The old house continued in use. This fort was lived in for a considerable period, and was frequently repaired and modified.

*Clickhimin: the blockhouse built inside the fort.*

***Clickhimin*** *from above.*

*Clickhimin: the approach causeway and outer defences.*

Perhaps around 100 BC, an attempt was made to upgrade the defences. A large masonry "blockhouse" with a hollow interior and a narrow entrance was erected immediately inside the original fort's gateway. This may have been a temporary expedient, for almost immediately work began on a major sub-circular masonry structure within the enclosure. This shows signs of hasty work, and it was abandoned incomplete, to be used instead as the base for a low circular tower, or broch.

The broch at **Clickhimin** has been somewhat rebuilt, particularly in 1861 when it was "investigated by some gentlemen of Lerwick". But it is probably not far from its original height of around 10 m. It takes the form of a solid ring of masonry, 5 m thick, surrounding an inner courtyard 10 m across. Access is through a low, narrow passage, in which there survive checks for a wooden door-frame and, on the right-hand side, the possible trace of a walled-up cell or guard-post. Within, the earthen floor had a ring of wooden posts, presumably to support a raised floor and roof, the outer edges of which would have rested on narrow ledges, or scarcements, on the inner wall-face. Within the thickness of the upper wall are the typical galleries and stairway of a broch, giving access to the wallhead, while in the thickness of the wall's base are oval cells, perhaps store-rooms.

Later, the broch seems to have been abandoned as a defence; the wooden structures were removed and a loosely built inner casing of stone was added, reducing the floor area and converting the building into a single-family dwelling, which could no longer provide refuge for a large number of people. While this conversion was underway there is evidence for contact with outsiders, perhaps from Orkney, in the form of unusual pottery. The old Bronze-Age house was brought back into use during the building changes.

As time went by, even this modified dwelling was abandoned, and the last phases of use, perhaps around AD 500, saw the site occupied by a succession of smaller and rather flimsy houses, partly dug into the ruins. One of the oddest features, and perhaps of late date, is a curious stone slab with the outlines of two footprints carved into it. This sits across the original approach from the causeway. Elsewhere in Celtic Europe such stones are often traditionally associated either with legends of saints or with kingship as at **Dunadd**, ancient capital of the Scots, in mid-Argyll; but there are no such traditions associated with the **Clickhimin** stone.

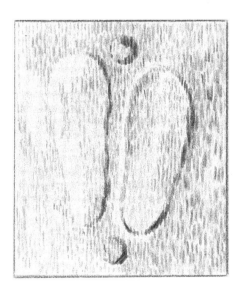 

*Clickhimin: the footprint slab.*

ontrasting sharply with **Clickhimin**, both in its setting and in its complexity, is the fort at **Ness of Burgi**, situated on an exposed headland near the southernmost tip of Shetland. Here a double ditch and bank, the latter once stone-faced, cuts off a small promontory. Access to the interior is by a stone-lined passageway which may have been roofed, though it is now too ruined for us to be certain.

*HU 387084*
*Park considerate*
*on the narrow*
*road.*
*1 mile from the*
*road end with a*
*rocky scramble*
*near the end.*

Within this defensive line is a large rectangular masonry "blockhouse", similar in general plan to the one at **Clickhimin** but somewhat lower. Inside it are two oval cells and the ruins of a third, one being entered from the entrance passage and another from the rear. Although no trace of post-holes was found, it may be assumed that there was once a timber-framed structure leaning against the rear of the masonry block, as seems to have been the case at **Clickhimin**.

Some scholars take the view that blockhouses represent an early form of fortification, ancestral to brochs, in which some of the ideas later incorporated in brochs, such as the high, hollow wall and the narrow entrance passage, were first developed. However, the balance of evidence favours the idea that forts which incorporate blockhouses were broadly contemporary with the brochs. In most cases they are built in areas which are poorer in agricultural terms; they may therefore possibly have belonged to groups of people who had less time and labour to devote to constructing a defence.

Even so, a cliff-edged promontory defended as at **Ness of Burgi** would have presented a formidable aspect. The stone-faced ramparts would have stood higher, pierced only by a single narrow entrance, holding unknown hazards. Behind the rampart would have risen the blockhouse, providing a platform for spearmen or slingers, so that even if the rampart were stormed the ground between it and the blockhouse would form a "killing ground", overlooked by the defenders on the wallhead. Such forts represented an economical way of providing an impressive defence for a relatively small group, and probably belonged to the poorer relations of the broch-builders.

**Ness of Burgi**: *the fort clings to the top of low cliffs.*

**Ness of Burgi**:
*the ditch on the landward side.*

In 1983 a ruined fort a short distance to the north of **Ness of Burgi** was excavated, revealing the surviving half of a blockhouse similar in dimensions to the one at **Ness of Burgi**, protected by a landward rampart. It is not known if this was a sister fort, a predecessor, or an ancestor. The whole question of the building date of brochs and forts is still under review, as new excavations take place.

*The **Clickhimin** blockhouse reconstructed–*
***Ness of Burgi** would have looked similar.*

*I 457236
:ess by private
·t from Sand
·dge pier.
ephone
·dwick 367.*

**B**y the end of the broch-building period, about AD 100, brochs and forts may have
become symbols of status for their owners, rather than strictly necessary as defences.
From these last years may date the best preserved broch in all Scotland, that which
stands on the uninhabited island of **Mousa**.

**Mousa** can be reached by boat from Sand Lodge pier in South Mainland. From the landing-
place a short walk over the shoulder of the hill gives a fine view of this impressive structure,
one of the supreme examples of drystone building technique in prehistoric Scotland.

The broch is a little smaller in diameter than most, and its walls are proportionately thicker.
This solid foundation may have allowed it to be built a little taller than most brochs, so its
13.3 m may be exceptional. The entrance, along a narrow passage which has lost its original
roofing slabs, leads into an interior cluttered by stonework of later sub-divisions (see page 17).
A water tank, cut down to bedrock, appears original. The tower is constructed of flagstones
quarried on the nearby shore. Its solid base contains three oval cells, but from a height of 3 m

the wall is hollow, containing six superimposed galleries floored
and roofed with large slabs. A stair of narrow stone steps rises
through these galleries to the wallhead, which retains part of its
original capping, a slanting slabbed roof. Vertical apertures in
the inner wall-face allow light into the galleries; they also reduce
the weight of the structure and may once have allowed access
from the stone part of the broch to at least two wooden floors
within it. These floors were carried on posts set into the floor and
supported at their outer edge by ledges, or scarcements,
protruding from the inner wall-face. Higher up, large protruding
blocks may have helped anchor a wooden roof.

***Mousa Broch** today stands over 13 m tall, and from outside looks much as it
would have in the Iron Age.*

The galleries in the wall thickness were largely a constructional device, lightening the weight and acting as a rising scaffolding as building progressed. Once completed they were of little use except for storage, since it would have been necessary to place a ladder across the stair to enter them. It may be that even the stairway leading to the wallhead saw little use except for those on lookout duty. Access to the central wooden roundhouse, in which daily life was conducted, would normally have been by timber ladders or stairways, now long-vanished.

From the top of the broch, a sweeping view would have allowed warning of any approaching attacker. Interestingly, the wall is carried just high enough to allow a view out to the east, across the low middle part of the island. There are other examples in Shetland of brochs, now ruined, that would also have allowed their defenders to peer out cautiously to sea across intervening land.

As at **Clickhimin**, the defensive qualities of **Mousa** were later compromised by the removal of the wooden elements and the construction within the courtyard of a smaller-diameter structure of stone. This might have housed a single family of descendants of the broch-builders, but would not have had space to accommodate the rest of the local community in times of danger. Outside the broch, a low wall probably represents an enclosure for stock. There were once traces of small houses near the entrance to the broch, but these have now been almost entirely removed by the sea.

As late as AD 900 the broch was still defensible, for around that year an eloping couple took shelter in "Moseyarborg" (the name means "bird-island-fort") when their ship was wrecked there en route from Norway to Iceland. A similar escapade in AD 1153 saw the broch put in a state to withstand the pursuit of Earl Harold Maddadson, who was seeking to recover his mother from an adventurer called Erland. The Earl's men found the broch "an unhandy place to get at". Fortunately, for future visitors, this episode was settled without any attempt being made to take the broch by siege or assault. But by these chance events, **Mousa** became one of the few clearly identifiable locations in Shetland to be mentioned in the Norse sagas, and Shetland moved, tentatively, into recorded history.

*Inside **Mousa**: entrance and openings in the inner wall-face.*

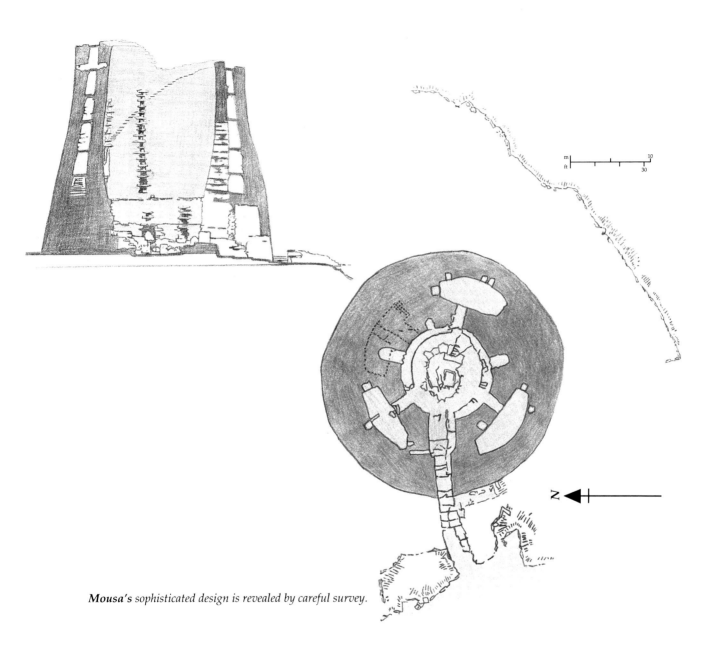

*Mousa's* sophisticated design is revealed by careful survey.

In the second century AD brochs went out of use as defences. It is not known whether some new means of warfare rendered them obsolete, whether the threats against which they had been built disappeared, or whether social conditions changed so that defence was no longer necessary. One attractive explanation would see the Roman defeat of the inhabitants of north-east Scotland at Mons Graupius in AD 84 as having removed the main external threat to the broch-builders, but this theory is hard to test by archaeology. Whatever the reasons, brochs ceased to be built, and were replaced by lower circular dwellings, known to archaeologists as wheelhouses, and designed to accommodate a single family. Fine examples can be seen at **Jarlshof**. Probably the leading families lived in these new-style dwellings, within or near to the brochs, while the rest of the local agricultural population dispersed, as in pre-broch days, to build farmhouses near to their land. Only a handful of these dwellings have been found; they seem to have been simple round houses, rather like the hut-circles found in areas further south.

As time passed, the elaborate wheelhouses also went out of fashion and were replaced by simpler structures. The architecture of the late Iron Age in Shetland gives an impression of gradually increasing poverty, though this could, in part, be due to changes in construction: perhaps turf or even imported timber were now being used as the main constructional materials and so do not survive in the way that stone buildings do. In any case, for the period around the end of the Iron Age and the start of the Dark Ages, about AD 500, it is hard to identify any houses, and only one burial is known.

*Shetland's only Pictish burial place: excavations at Sandwick on Unst in 1978.*

*Jarlshof: a wheelhouse dwelling of the later Iron Age.*

# *Pictish Shetland*

The absence of archaeological evidence for Shetland around AD 500 is particularly vexing because it is precisely at this period that the islands enter what may be called the proto-historic period, and some very limited information begins to be available about events elsewhere in Scotland. At some time the islands, along with Orkney, were absorbed into the Pictish kingdom, or at least that kingdom's sphere of influence. A small number of well-carved stones, in the Pictish style, reveal by their motifs that by about AD 700 there were Christians in the population; indeed by then the whole population may have been Christian.

Who converted the Shetlanders? Churches sited in places such as Papil on West Burra, Cullingsburgh on Bressay and St Ninian's Isle suggest a parish structure established in the

*Sheep on the magnificent beach linking St Ninian's Isle to Mainland.*

heart of the best farmland, and apparently serving the local people. On the other hand a series of remote, often perilous, hermitages seem to have been established on headlands and rock stacks. This does not resolve the question of whether the initial Christianising influence came from the south-west, through the Irish followers of Columba, or from the more Northumbrian-oriented Pictish church, since both traditions carried out their work through missionary churches or monasteries in the midst of the lay population as well as in lonely retreats for prayer and spiritual refreshment.

Although there are no surviving defences from this period (indeed, some of the hermitages are located within abandoned forts ) there must, none the less, have been tension. Viking raiders from Norway, who are recorded further south, must have called in at Shetland, and probably over-wintered there too. The alarm caused by one such visit may be the explanation for the magnificent collection of eighth-century Pictish silverware that was found in 1958 below the floor of the ruined twelfth-century church on St Ninian's Isle. Was this the property of a churchman, hidden and never retrieved? - or the loot of a raider hidden from his colleagues who took a savage revenge? Certainly the richness of this treasure sits oddly in a period when Shetland, if no longer in constant fear of conflict, was apparently going through an unexplained period of decline.

*A small selection of the rich hoard of Pictish treasure found on St Ninian's Isle (reproduced by permission of the Trustees of the National Museums of Scotland).*

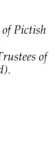

round AD 800, when the remarkable wave of Viking settlement began throughout the North Atlantic seaboard, Shetland was settled early, before Orkney, the Hebrides and Caithness. There is unfortunately no saga record of the settlement of Shetland, as there is for Iceland. This is a great lack, for nothing survives to explain the success of the Norse invaders over what seems to have been a demoralised or numerically much-reduced population. Place-name evidence shows that the Celtic language was swept aside by the Norsemen, who set about renaming everything, including the islands themselves, which became Hjaltland, probably meaning "the high land". A few place-names, often in remote areas, such as Pettaster, Pettifirth and Pettadale, hint at the continued presence of Picts, while the "papa" names, such as Papil and Papa Stour, suggest that the incomers found Celtic priests in residence. These seem to have been tolerated but failed to convert many of the pagan Norsemen - it took a visit from King Olaf Tryggvason to Earl Sigurd in AD 995 to achieve this, at the point of the sword.

*A Viking ship: graffito from **Jarlshof**.*

*Looking towards Papa Stour, the "big island of priests".*

Only one site of the early Viking settlement period has been extensively excavated, that at **Jarlshof** (see below p. 37). Apart from **Jarlshof**, Norse houses, whether of the settlement period or later, are singularly hard to locate in Shetland. Only at Sandwick and Underhoull on Unst have longhouses been excavated, while at Gossabrough on Yell and Strandibrough on Fetlar there are convincing unexcavated examples. Place-name evidence, however, suggests a large-scale, rapid colonisation. The key to the apparent scarcity of Norse farms may lie in the fact that, because the way of life has changed little in Shetland until recently, their remains now lie below modern crofts, which have been rebuilt on the same sites over the centuries. In a region where good farmland is at a premium, it would have made good sense to re-use existing farm sites. Indeed, even the first Norse settlers recognised this, building on the mound of rubble at **Jarlshof** which by then already contained the debris from over 2000 years of human settlement.

One very distinctive building type which was introduced at this time was the "Norse" mill, a small variety of corn-mill powered by water, with a direct drive from a horizontal paddle-wheel to the upper of two small millstones. Such mills remained in use until early in the twentieth century, and their ruins now dot many small watercourses.

*Ruined "Norse" mill, Loch of Clumlie.*

During the centuries after the first land-taking, Shetland became a part of the emerging Norse Earldom of Orkney, and at various times played a role in its troubled history. Harald Finehair, King of Norway, who effectively established the Earldom around AD 890, anchored his fleet in the Unst bay which now bears his name, "Haroldswick". Shetland was also used as a staging post by Norwegian Earls and Kings on their way to attempt great deeds, and sometimes on their return following defeat. But throughout this period it was increasingly subordinated to the more prosperous islands of Orkney to the south, so that while later sagas and histories speak often of Orkney, little is known of Shetland.

From the scant references and later evidence, it is possible to draw a picture of late Norse society in Shetland, around AD 1400. By this time the Earl, though still subject to Norway, was a Scot. He held considerable lands, as did the Church. But outwith these lands there was a large class of land-holders who held their land in their own right, without owing any personal service or dues to the Earl. These land-holders, or "udallers", in turn let their land to a larger class of tenant-farmers. Both tenants and proprietors normally employed labourers, who also worked small plots for their own household needs.

There was a codified legal system, and a number of local assemblies, known as "tings", met to decide points of ownership or minor illegalities. The districts of these parliaments gave rise to some of the present parish names: Aithsting (the parliament of the isthmus), Nesting (..of the headland), Delting ( . . of the valley), and so on. An annual gathering of representatives from the local tings met at the Law Ting Holm, in Tingwall (parliament valley), to settle weightier matters. Although in theory open to all freemen it seems likely that the Shetland parliament, like those of other Norse-colonised areas such as the Isle of Man or Iceland, was controlled by the most powerful land-owners and chief among them the Earl or his nominees.

*Law Ting Holm, open-air site of Shetland's parliament.*

*Tingwall kirkyard, on the site of Shetland's principal pre-Reformation church.*

*Shetland's first castle? Loch of Strom.*

It is interesting to note how close together the chief places of late Norse Shetland are: only a few miles separate Scalloway (where the the chief harbour is traditionally assumed to have been), the Law Ting Holm, and the church at Tingwall, where a neat eighteenth-century building overlies the foundations of the principal church of medieval Shetland, in which the Archdeacon had his seat. Not far away, in the Loch of Strom, sits the ruin of what may be Shetland's earliest castle, dating from the late fourteenth or early fifteenth century. Somewhat oddly, the Earl's residence was in the extreme south of the islands, at Sumburgh, but this location may have much to do with the distribution of agricultural land owned directly by the Earldom.

HU 398095
Parking at
Sumburgh
Airport Hotel.
Admission fee.

The large mound covering the Iron-Age and earlier remains at **Jarlshof** was partly occupied by a Pictish farming family when it was acquired by an immigrant family from south-west Norway early in the ninth century AD. How the acquisition took place is not clear, although a degree of compulsion seems likely for the surrounding farmland is some of Shetland's richest.

The first Norse settlers built a large longhouse, with slightly bowed side walls. It was probably mainly of turf with a stone footing, and roofed with straw ropes and heather thatch. The house had a spacious main room, combining living and sleeping space, and a small kitchen at one end. Outbuildings, including a barn and a byre, stood near by. One small building may have been a simple temple, for at this date the incomers would have been pagans, worshipping the Norse gods.

As years passed, the original house was altered. The kitchen was moved into the centre, and the east wall was removed and a large byre added. At the same time a number of other farm buildings and houses were built, as the original single farm grew wealthier. The single farm became a small village. Now the inhabitants began increasingly to use the sea as a source of food. In addition to fish, wild birds, whales and seals gave variety to the daily diet as the settlers and their descendants came to know and exploit the full range of Shetland's resources.

A striking feature of the plan of Norse **Jarlshof**, observed elsewhere in the Atlantic settlements, is a change of orientation in the houses from NW-SE to NE-SW. This may indicate a relatively rapid change in the climate, with a swing in the prevailing winds - always a dominant feature in Shetland life. This change may have been a contributory factor to the weakening of links with the homeland in Norway which seems to have begun around the early fourteenth century.

It was at settlements such as **Jarlshof** that many of the features of recent Shetland rural life were established. Long rectangular houses, boat shelters ('noosts') on the shore, the vessels used for fishing and trading - all have their roots in the traditions brought by the new settlers.

*Viking or Pict? Sketch on slate from **Jarlshof**.*

For all its Norse tradition, however, Shetland was increasingly "Scottified" in the centuries before its formal annexation by Scotland in 1469. There was almost certainly limited immigration from Scotland from the eleventh century onwards, and this influx of people had its effect on the language, customs and farming practices of the islands.

At **Jarlshof** itself, the village was succeeded, around the end of the thirteenth century or beginning of the fourteenth, by a farmhouse with a parallel barn and detached byre - much more on the Scottish model. As the maritime power of Norway waned, so the importance of trading links with Scotland grew. From 1236 the Earl himself was a Scot, and in 1379 the Earldom came into the hands of the Sinclair family, with whom it would be associated for almost a century.

*Jarlshof: the earliest Norse longhouse.*

In 1469, King James III of Scotland married Margaret, the daughter of Christian I of Norway and Denmark. By the terms of the marriage agreement, the Princess was to bring with her a dowry of 60,000 florins. The royal estates in Orkney were handed over to the Scottish Crown as a pledge for 50,000 of these, but when, eight months later, the remainder had still not been paid, the 'kingslands' of Shetland were also pledged for a further 8,000 florins. The dowry never was paid in full, and although the possibility of Denmark redeeming the islands was still being raised as late as 1749, in effect from 1469 both Shetland and Orkney became part of Scotland.

As we have seen, connections between Shetland and Scotland had always been strong, to the extent that since 1236, the Earldom of Orkney, to which Shetland was attached, had been held by Scots. In 1470 James III annexed the Earldom by buying out Earl William Sinclair and granting him in return a pension and the castle of **Ravenscraig**, in Fife. Earl William's grandson, Lord Henry Sinclair, later continued the tradition of family prominence in the islands by serving the King as tacksman, or lessee of the island revenues; but, after his death alongside James IV on Flodden field in 1513, the family, torn apart by internal feuding, gradually lost its position in the islands to incomers from the south.

When the Earldom was re-established in 1581, it was to a family of incomers, albeit royally connected, that it was granted. Robert Stewart (1533-93) was an illegitimate son of James V. His interests in the Northern Isles began in 1564, when he was granted the feu of the royal and Earldom estates of Orkney and Shetland, together with the office of Sheriff.

*Queen Margaret, daughter of Christian I of Denmark, and James III, as they appear on the altarpiece of Trinity Church, Edinburgh, painted by Hugo Van der Goes.* (Reproduced by gracious permission of Her Majesty the Queen.)

*The **Earl's Palace**, built by Earl Patrick c. 1606 in the precincts of the former **Bishop's Palace** in **Kirkwall**, Orkney.*

Four years later, he also acquired the former Bishopric lands from the Bishop of Orkney, Adam Bothwell, and from Bothwell's cousin, Sir John Bellenden. Complaints about the harshness of his administration, however, found a willing listener in Regent Morton, and resulted in 1575 in a brief imprisonment for him in **Edinburgh Castle**. But in 1578, Robert was back in Orkney, and, after Morton's death, he was appointed Earl of Orkney and Lord of Shetland, in 1581. The islanders' complaints continued, however, and to them was now added the opposition of the dispossessed Bellendens. Although Robert was to die peacefully in the former **Bishop's Palace** in **Kirkwall** in 1593, this was only after he had defeated an armed expedition, led by Sir Patrick Bellenden of Stenness, sent to fetch him back to stand trial in Edinburgh.

Earl Robert was succeeded by his son, Patrick Stewart, who was already being styled Earl of Orkney (1592) and Lord of Shetland (1591) before his father's death. The income that Earl Patrick derived from his island estates and his willingness to run up enormous debts put him in an entirely different class from the other landowners in Orkney and Shetland. Their resentment of him was further increased both by his ostentatious lifestyle and by his habitual recourse to violence as a means of settling disputes. In 1597, for instance, he seized **Noltland Castle** on Westray, in Orkney, with a force of 60 men, in order, so it was said, to recover a debt owed him by the owner, Michael Balfour. In 1608, he made similar attempts on **Muness Castle** and on Sumburgh House (**Jarlshof**), in Shetland, making off with £8,346 Scots worth of goods from the latter belonging to William Bruce of Symbister. Patrick's other local opponents included Robert Monteath of Egilsay, and the Sinclairs of Eday, whose quarry had provided the stone for his palace in **Kirkwall**.

In 1605, James Law was installed as Bishop of Orkney, and with the blessing of James VI, set out to curb Earl Patrick's power. This was not easy, but by March 1609 Patrick had made so many enemies and was so impoverished financially that he was forced to leave for Edinburgh. There he was imprisoned for a while, before being taken to **Dumbarton Castle**. The following year, an attempt to bring him to trial for treason came to nothing; but despite this and other devices intended to induce him to resign his Earldom, Patrick refused, prevaricated and plotted, while his followers continued to cause unrest in the islands. In May 1614, however, while Patrick was still awaiting trial in **Dumbarton Castle**, his illegitimate son, Robert, landed in Orkney, seized **Birsay Palace**, and with the Earl's supporters proceeded to take the castle and **Bishop's Palace** in **Kirkwall**. The revolt was finally suppressed by the Earl of Caithness in September 1614. The young Robert Stewart was hanged in Edinburgh on 5 January 1615, and his father, Patrick, was beheaded a month later.

*The Old House of Sumburgh (**Jarlshof**), built by Earl Patrick and feued to William Bruce of Symbister in 1592.*

# Muness Castle: Britain's northernmost castle

L aurence Bruce, the builder of **Muness Castle**, was one of the more notorious of the Scottish incomers to Shetland in the later sixteenth century. A native of Cultmalindie in Perthshire, he was also half-brother to Robert Stewart, Earl of Orkney. He probably accompanied Robert on the latter's expedition to Orkney in 1569, and in 1573 he was appointed *foud*, sheriff-depute and chamberlain of the Lordship lands of Shetland, and bailie, justiciary and chamberlain of the lands of the Bishopric.

HU 629012
On Unst.
Ferry from Y

A detailed account of Bruce's corrupt and oppressive administration as *foud*, or sheriff, is set out in the list of *Complaints* that were made by local people to the Privy Council's commissioners at a series of hearings held throughout the islands in February 1577. These included Bruce's replacement of elected *lawrightmen* by his own bailiffs, and his use of faulty weights and measures in assessing the payments of the tax *(skat)* that the Shetlanders had to make in coarse cloth *(wadmell)*, butter and oil (obtained from fish and other sea creatures). Like his half-brother, Bruce weathered this storm; but he did not thereafter enjoy such power, and his position was eclipsed altogether when Patrick Stewart succeeded his father as Earl and as Lord of Shetland in the 1590s. Considerable ill-feeling developed between the two, and even before Patrick had begun to build **Scalloway Castle**, Bruce was constructing for himself a castle at **Muness**, on the northerly island of Unst. An inscription over the doorway gives the year of commencement as 1598. It is likely that the Earl's own mason, John Ross, who witnessed the delivery of letters of horning (outlawry) against Laurence Bruce on 21 July 1604, would have had a hand in its construction, and its similarities with **Scalloway**, though on a reduced scale, may also betray the influence of Andrew Crawford, Earl Patrick's master of works.

Laurence Bruce had good reason to feel the need for a secure residence, for in 1608 Earl Patrick landed on Unst with 36 men, intent on punishing him for having assisted another of the Earl's personal enemies. The landing party included the Earl's trumpeters and fiddler, besides his master-gunner, who came equipped with a battery of brass and iron cannon. But before the castle's defences could be put to the test, the would-be attackers unexpectedly withdrew.

**Muness Castle**, *seen from the SE.*

In 1617, seven years before he died, Laurence Bruce bestowed **Muness** on his second son, Andrew. In 1627, the castle was attacked, this time by Dunkirk privateers, who burnt it along with Andrew Bruce's writs. The letters "A.B.", which could at the time be seen below the south-west turret, may possibly have related to a subsequent phase of repairs. By the end of the century, however, the castle was no longer inhabited.

In 1713, following the wreck of the *Rynenburgh*, the building was leased for four months to the Dutch East India Company for storage of the ship's salvaged cargo. Five years later, the Bruce family sold it. At that time its contents amounted to no more than a parcel of old pewter, one small brewing kettle, a parcel of old leather, and some wooden chairs. Archaeological excavation of the floors in the main hall and north-east tower in 1975 indicated that the building was finally abandoned around 1750. By 1774, it was already roofless.

*Muness Castle* from the SW, showing the elaborately corbelled SW turret.

*Brass door-knocker from **Muness Castle**, bearing the name "Andro Brus" above the quartered arms of his parents, Laurence Bruce and Elizabeth Gray, and the motto "Omnia fincit amor" (Love conquers all things).*

he castle is built to the so-called Z-plan design, but with cylindrical rather than rectangular towers at the diagonally opposing corners, and rounded turrets corbelled out high up on the other two. Between them, these towers and turrets would have enabled gunners, shooting through the gun-loops below the windows, to cover every part of the castle's external wall.

The entrance is on the south. The original doorway was lost before the building was taken into State care, but in 1959 the present eighteenth-century doorway was obtained from an abandoned house at Old Lund. Above it, in their original positions, are the Bruce coat of arms and an inscription in Gothic lettering, which reads:

> *LIST YE TO KNAW THIS BULDING QUHA BEGAN*
> *LAURENCE THE BRUCE HE WAS THAT WORTHY MAN*
> *QUHA ERNESTLY HIS AIRIS AND OFSPRING PRAYIS*
> *TO HELP AND NOT TO HURT THIS WARK ALUAYIS*
> *THE YEIR OF GOD. 1598.*

*The inscription over the entrance, surmounted by the Bruce coat of arms.*

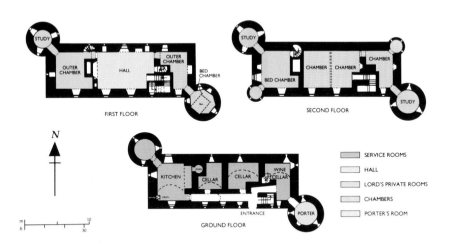

*The floor plans of **Muness Castle**.*

The basement of the castle contains four dark vaulted rooms linked by a narrow vaulted corridor. Most of these rooms, as well as the ground floors of the corner-towers, were probably used for storage, and a narrow service stair leads up from the eastern room into the great hall. The western room, at the far end of the corridor, was evidently the kitchen. It has a fireplace containing a bread oven on the east, a slop-drain in the south-west corner, and a doorway (now blocked) in the north wall for bringing in supplies from outside.

The main stair is to the right of the principal doorway, and in design represents a miniaturised version of the grand staircase built at roughly the same time at **Scalloway Castle**. It leads directly into the hall on the first floor. In 1975, excavation revealed that the hall was originally paved with irregular stone flags but that sometime in the early eighteenth century the earlier paving was overlain by a timber floor supported on timber joists. The walls were probably panelled in timber, and the wooden ceiling enlivened by painted decoration. The windows in the north and south walls have gun-loops below their sills; and an ample fireplace is set in the west wall.

*The hall, with the door to Laurence Bruce's private apartment to the right of the fireplace.*

A small doorway to the right of the fireplace leads into the owner's private apartment. This was on two levels, with a spiral stair communicating between them. The lower room served as an outer chamber or withdrawing room, and the upper one as Bruce's bedchamber. It was evidently considered unnecessary to have a fireplace in the lower room, which would have received adequate heat from the kitchen below. Each room communicated with a small closet, or "study", in the north-west tower, and the upper room with the projecting south-western turret; it may have been in one of these studies that Andrew Bruce was keeping his writs, when they were burnt in 1627.

*The staircase within Bruce's private apartment.*

The way into the other chambers of the castle was from the opposite, or "lower", end of the hall. From here a door leads through a roughly L-shaped room, containing a fireplace, into an octagonal room inside the south-east corner-tower. This too contains a fireplace, three windows (with shot-holes below them), and on the south-west a recess indicating the position for a bed. Despite their unusual shapes, these two rooms seem to have formed an independent suite, comprising an inner and an outer chamber, dependent on the hall.

To reach the other chambers, one had to return once more to the hall and proceed up the main staircase. Unfortunately the layout of the second floor is not entirely certain. Possibly the space above the hall was divided into two rooms, one with its own fireplace and the other receiving its heat from the combined kitchen and hall chimney, while a third chamber, also with a fireplace, occupied the space above the L-shaped room. This upper L-shaped room also communicated with rounded closets or studies in the south-east tower and north-east turret.

In its heyday the castle would have been surrounded by subsidiary buildings, courtyards and gardens. Some traces of these may still be seen in the rises and depressions of the ground in the field to the south.

The Scottish Earls of Orkney seem to have taken little personal interest in the dependent Lordship of Shetland before the time of Earl Patrick in the 1590s. Most of the wealth of the Earldom lay, after all, in the rich farming lands of Orkney. Tingwall, however, in the central part of mainland Shetland, continued to be the principal meeting place for the court, presided over by the *foud*, or sheriff. When Earl Patrick decided to build himself a fortified residence in Shetland to match the now-lost castle in Kirkwall, a site near Tingwall was therefore a natural place for him to choose.

HU 404392
*In Scalloway.*

*The doorway to Scalloway Castle, surmounted by the royal arms and Patrick Stewart's inscription, dated AD 1600.*

**Scalloway Castle** stands 4.75 km (3 miles) south of the Law Ting Holm of Tingwall, on a low natural promontory surrounded originally by the sea on three sides. The houses, wharfs and jetties of the town of Scalloway would have extended around the bay to the west. Although all that remains of the castle today is the principal tower-house, containing the Earl's hall and apartment, it may be assumed that when first built its ancillary buildings and yards would have extended over the whole peninsula. The date of construction is given by an inscription above the main door, which in the eighteenth century could still be read as follows:

*PATRICIVS STEVARDVS ORCHADIAE ET ZETLANDIAE*
*COMES. I. V. R. S.*
*CUJUS FVNDAMEN SAXVM EST DOM'ILLA MANEBIT*
*LABILIS E CONTRA SI SIT ARENA PERIT*
*A. D. 1600*

*Patrick Stewart, Earl of Orkney and Shetland. James V(I), King of Scots.*
*That house whose foundation is rock will stand,*
*but will perish if it be shifting sand.*
*AD 1600*

**Scalloway Castle**, *seen from the harbour to the SW.*

49

If this piece of bad Latin verse was intended to portray Earl Patrick as the "wise man" of Matthew 8.24, it missed its mark, for though the castle remains, his own fall was great indeed (cf Luke 6.59). The man in charge of the building work may have been Andrew Crawford, "sumtym servant and maister of vark to the Erle of Orknay", whose tombstone, dated 160[-], lies in Tingwall churchyard; the Earl's mason, John Ross, was also doubtless employed on it.

The claims made by Earl Patrick's enemies that he forced local people to contribute labour and materials to his building works finds some support in the Court Book of Shetland. In 1602, for example, we read that John Cauldbak was made to pay £10 for disobeying the sheriff's orders, "in non passing in to my lordis wark to Skalloway as he was derectit". In August of the same year, Earl Patrick himself presided over a court session held in the castle, which dealt amongst other matters with the question of the weights and measures used by German, or "Dutch", merchants trading with Shetland. Other cases, heard over the next two years, concerned the illegal retention by the townsfolk of Scalloway of driftwood, which belonged as of right to the King, and the theft of the Earl's peats; indeed, a rental of 1604 records that the inhabitants of various Shetland parishes were to provide 32 fathoms (over 4,000 m³) of peat for **Scalloway Castle** each year. Evidently the castle was a large place to keep even tolerably warm!

After Earl Patrick's downfall in 1609, **Scalloway Castle** continued to be used for local administration and justice. In 1612-13, the King's commissioner, Bishop James Law, is recorded holding court there in the great hall. And a gruesome reminder of the nature of justice dispensed is given by an item of expenditure, recorded in 1640, for a new axe for the "maiden", or beheading machine.

The castle was still habitable during the period of the Commonwealth in the 1650s, when English soldiers were quartered in and about it. Around 1695, Martin Martin noted that "several rooms have been curiously painted, though the better part be now worn off". At the end of the century, however, it was reported that the roof was letting in water and the timber beginning to rot. In 1754, the Earl of Morton permitted Sir Andrew Mitchell to remove much of the softer freestone for reuse in his mansion house at Sand. As late as 1733, however, Thomas Gifford had noted that all public letters were still being executed in **Scalloway Castle**, even though by then the head courts were commonly held in Lerwick.

In 1908, the Marquis of Zetland placed the castle in the guardianship of the State and extensive consolidation works were carried out, including the building up in new masonry of the collapsed lower vaults and other unstable portions.

The main tower house, which is all that remains of **Scalloway Castle** today, stands three storeys high (not counting the loft) above a vaulted ground floor. Its plan is rectangular, with a square block, or "jamb", projecting at the south-west corner, containing the entrance and main stair. Above the doorway is a panel bearing a now-illegible inscription (see page 48), and above this two empty frames intended to contain heraldic panels, surmounted by a much-weathered representation of the royal arms.

The tower-house was a self-contained residence. Indeed, except that its rooms are arranged on four floors instead of three, its layout is remarkably similar to that of the palace block that Earl Patrick built for himself in Kirkwall a few years later. As at Kirkwall, the ground floor is taken up by service rooms. To the left of the entrance, a small room below the stairs would have been used by the porter or door-keeper, and also as a temporary lock-up for miscreants awaiting a court hearing in the hall upstairs. It was here, in "the laich volt of the jame", that Henry Wardlaw, a servant of Laurence Bruce, was held in August 1602. To the right, a vaulted passage gives access to two rooms below the main tower. The one at the far end (which now contains an introductory display) was probably simply a storage cellar. The other is the kitchen. This contains a well, which earlier this century still supplied water to nearby houses. The fireplace occupied the whole western end of the room; its arch has now gone, but the massive chimney flue may still be seen, rising the full height of the tower.

*Scalloway Castle from the NE, showing the corbelled stair-turret leading up to the Earl's private apartment.*

*The decorative corbelling below the NE stair-turret, including false gunloops to deter the overinquisitive.*

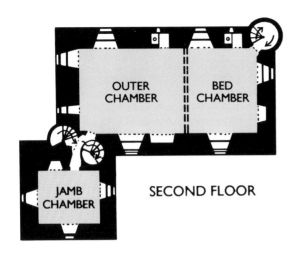

**SECOND FLOOR**

OUTER CHAMBER

BED CHAMBER

JAMB CHAMBER

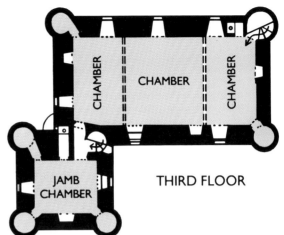

**THIRD FLOOR**

CHAMBER

CHAMBER

CHAMBER

JAMB CHAMBER

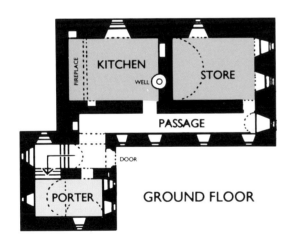

**GROUND FLOOR**

FIREPLACE

KITCHEN

WELL

STORE

PASSAGE

DOOR

PORTER

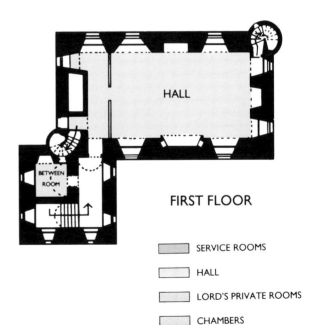

**FIRST FLOOR**

HALL

BETWEEN ROOM

*N*

m — 10
ft — 30

SERVICE ROOMS

HALL

LORD'S PRIVATE ROOMS

CHAMBERS

PORTER/STEWARD'S ROOM

*53*

Important persons, however, would not have dallied at this level of the castle, but would have proceeded straight across the entrance vestibule and up the grand staircase. The design of this stair breaks with the earlier, medieval tradition of spiral stairs, such as is still found for example at **Noltland Castle** in Orkney, and ascends instead by means of short straight flights of steps, interspersed with landings, in a manner known as "scale-and-platt". To the left of the final landing, just before the entrance to the hall, a small doorway (remade in 1908) opens into a tiny square chamber, equipped with a fireplace and a window. This was the "between room", occupied by the Earl's steward, who ran the household and controlled access to the great hall.

The great hall occupies the entire first floor of the tower-house. The door from the stair leads into its "lower" end, which originally would have been partitioned off from the rest by a timber screen. Apart from cutting out draughts, this also provided a serving area between the kitchen and the hall. The Earl would have sat at the opposite, or "upper" end of the hall, directly in front of the fire in the end wall. A second fireplace, in the south wall, provided more general heating for the body of the room, while opposite it, in the north wall, an arched recess would probably have contained a buffet (or dresser) on which the household silver was displayed.

*The great hall as it might have looked in the time of Earl Patrick – and as it is today.*

When not being used for court hearings, banquets or other formal functions, the hall served - like the "hallway" of a modern house - as the main central space from which the other more private rooms of the house were accessible. The timber floors and partitions of the upper stories have now disappeared, but it is still possible to tell where they were from indications left on the standing walls. Immediately above the great hall were two rooms, one roughly twice the size of the other. The larger room, on the west, was the Earl's "outer chamber" (or "dining room" as the equivalent room is called in the palace at Kirkwall). This would have led into the smaller room, the Earl's bedchamber. Each room was provided with a latrine closet and a fireplace. Access to the outer chamber was from the narrow spiral stair which leads off from the lower end of the great hall; the Earl, however, had a more direct route to his bedchamber, up another stair which starts from the hall's north-east corner.

Above the Earl's apartment, the third floor contained three chambers. Each had a fireplace, and the eastern one, entered from the Earl's private stair, also had a latrine closet. This and the chamber on the west also had access to the projecting turrets, or "rounds", at the north-west and south-east corners of the building.

In addition to the chambers in the tower-house's main block, there were also a further two chambers, possibly forming a suite, situated in the jamb above the grand staircase. These were both reached up the stair from the lower end of the hall. At the head of this stair is a landing, between the door to the Earl's outer chamber on the left and the lower of the two chambers in the jamb on the right. Unfortunately, when this part of the castle was rebuilt in 1908, the door to the latter was remade too far to the east. Some imagination is therefore required to visualise the spiral staircase continuing up clockwise in the space between the tower and the jamb, giving access to the upper levels of both. Each of the jamb chambers has a fireplace, and the upper one has a latrine closet and three projecting turrets.

*Scalloway Castle* from the SW.

B y the end of the sixteenth century, it was usual for a large Dutch fishing fleet to gather each summer in Bressay Sound, on the eastern side of Shetland, to follow the shoals of herring on their great migration. Shetlanders would set up booths along the shoreline, around which a lively trade took place, with local products being exchanged for imported leather goods, brandy and tobacco. These activities caused consternation to the authorities, as much for their loss of revenue as for the questionable nature of some of the goods on sale. In August 1615, for instance, the sheriff-depute William Livingston ordered that no one should resort to Bressay Sound to sell beer to the Hollanders, upon pain of a £20 fine, and that the owners of houses there should demolish them; furthermore, that no women should go there to sell socks or buy necessities for the seamen, but should send their sons, husbands or servants instead. The meaning of the last clause was clarified in November 1625, when Sheriff Sir John Buchanan ratified Livingston's act and ordered that the houses of beer sellers and prostitutes in Lerwick were to be demolished. It was from such beginnings that the town of Lerwick came into being.

It was not only Dutch fishermen, however, who made use of the sheltered anchorage of Bressay Sound in the early seventeenth century. Dutch East Indiamen returning laden with exotic goods from the Far East often preferred to risk the natural hazards of the northern route around Britain, than the more predictable dangers of French – and English – warships and privateers in the English Channel. As they passed from the Atlantic to the North Sea, these rich prizes would be met and escorted to their home ports by armed warships.

On three occasions in the seventeenth century Britain was at war with Holland. During the First Dutch War (1652-3), a fort seems to have been built at Lerwick to protect the ships of Cromwell's navy, but no trace of it survives. More is known of the fort built there at the time of the Second Dutch War (1665-7). Its commander was Captain William Sinclair, who sailed from Leith to Shetland in June 1665. The construction of the fort was placed in the hands of Charles II's master mason, Robert Milne, and is later reported (in 1733) to have cost £28,000 sterling. It was roughly pentagonal in shape, with a battery set behind a zig-zagged parapet wall facing out over the bay, and with angled bastions defending the landward sides. It contained a two-storey barrack block, holding 100 men, with space for another 200 to be quartered near by. However, a letter to the Earl of Lauderdale, Secretary for Scotland, in October 1666, reported that "the cannon they have are but smalle Gunns & the greatest but

demi culverines soe too smalle for the batteries towards the Sea or Sownd, neither have they balle ffor those they have". In July 1667, the rampart had still not been finished in stone, the question of water supply had not been resolved, and the fort was reckoned to be too large to be adequately defended by its garrison. At about the same time, the Treaty of Breda was signed with the Dutch, the fort's uselessness was finally recognised, and it was dismantled.

During the Third Dutch War, which lasted from 1672 to 1677, Lerwick was not garrisoned; but in 1673 the Dutch landed and burnt the fort's abandoned barrack block.

The fort was eventually completed a century later, when Britain found herself faced by the combined naval forces of France, Spain and the states of northern Europe during the conflict which resulted in the loss of most of her North American colonies (1776-83). The new fort was named after George III's Queen, Charlotte, and was garrisoned from March 1781 by 270 soldiers of the Earl of Sutherland's Regiment, commanded by Major James Sutherland. With a few minor additions, this is the **Fort Charlotte** that we see today.

*One of the guns used by the Royal Naval Reserve for practice at **Fort Charlotte** in the 1860s.*

*The south gate, **Fort Charlotte**, subsequently reduced in size to allow only pedestrian access.*

he ramparts of eighteenth-century **Fort Charlotte** follow the outline of the fort begun but left incomplete in 1665-7. They consist of a seaward battery for up to twelve guns and of bastioned defences to landward, enclosing the buildings of the fort. It is uncertain, however, whether the fort was ever completely finished before peace was declared at Versailles in 1783. Drawings made that year by Captain A. Frazer, the engineer responsible, show that a battery of eight 18-pounders and two heavy 9-pounders had been mounted to seaward, but that an additional two 68-pounders or 8-inch howitzers for the seaward battery and the full complement of 12-pounders for the landward bastions had not yet been installed. Between the bastions a timber platform, supported on masonry buttresses behind a parapet, was to provide a continuous wall-walk, along which soldiers armed with muskets could patrol the walls. On the seaward side, Frazer's plan also shows a series of walls, known as "traverses", which ran back at right angles to the outer wall; these were intended to prevent enemy guns from raking the whole length of the battery, but it is doubtful if they were ever built.

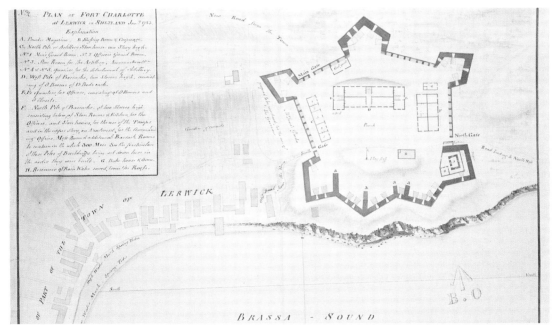

*A plan of **Fort Charlotte** drawn by Capt. A. Frazer, 1783. (Reproduced by permission of the Trustees of the National Library of Scotland).*

Otherwise, all the principal buildings shown on Frazer's plan still survive, though some have later modifications. In the centre of the fort, overlooking the parade ground, stands the "west pile" (today the Territorial Army hall and offices). This was originally a two-storey building throughout. The central block (D) contained eight barrack rooms, each for twenty six men sleeping in double beds, while the pavilions (E, E) at either end contained officers ' quarters, consisting in all of eight rooms with adjoining closets.

To the right (or north) of the "west pile" stands the "north pile" (F), also of two storeys. The ground floor of this building originally contained store rooms and the kitchen where the officers' meals were prepared; the men would have cooked their own food in the barrack rooms. On the upper floor were the apartment of the commanding officer, the officers' mess room, and an additional barrack room. To the west of this building, a small one-roomed out-house (G) was originally used as a bakehouse, and later on as a stable and then as a laundry.

To the left of the "west pile", the south side of the parade ground is flanked by a long low building (C), heavily modified since the eighteenth century and with an extension built on to its west end. The central part of this building contained the artillery and ammunition store. The two rooms to the west, towards the main gate, represented the guard rooms of the duty officers and men respectively, while another two on the east served as barrack rooms for the fort's specialist gunners.

In front of the "west pile", towards the north gate, is a low building (H) with a sloping roof. This encloses the brick-vaulted reservoir that held the fort's water supply. Rainwater was collected from the roofs of the other buildings and fed into it through a settling tank; the overflow from it was used to flush the latrines, situated just next to the north gate. Next to the latrines and enclosed by the fort's north-east bastion, stands the powder magazine (A), containing the

*The "north pile" (F), looking E with the original bakehouse (G) in the foreground.*

*Encroached on on almost every side by modern buildings, **Fort Charlotte's** distinctive pentagonal form is more easily appreciated from the air. In the background, **Clickhimin Broch** is a reminder of more distant conflicts.*

gunpowder supply for the fort's guns and muskets. This was carefully sited, so as to be conveniently near to the main battery, but as far as possible from the main buildings in case of an accidental explosion. Much attention was paid to ensuring that the gunpowder came to no harm, either through dampness or through its accidental ignition by flame, spark or enemy action. The magazine was therefore vaulted in brick, and its doors were double and made of timber with a copper covering. No iron was used in the building or in the kegs, in case of sparks. The air vents necessary to prevent condensation were dog-legged to stop shot or shrapnel penetrating inside. Because the men who worked in the magazine had to wear special shoes and clothing, a shifting room (B) was also provided, where they could change out of their normal uniforms; this small building also served as a cooperage, where empty kegs were stored and repaired.

Except for its inglorious burning in 1673, the fort has never seen enemy action throughout its 330-year history. When Britain went to war with Revolutionary France in 1793, a company of some 100 men of the newly formed Orkney and Shetland Fencibles were stationed in **Fort Charlotte** until 1797, when they were disbanded. They seem to have been replaced the following year by a new formation, the Shetland Fencibles, raised by Captain James Malcolmson; but this too was probably disbanded soon after 1814. The fort's eighteenth-century guns were removed in 1855, and between 1861 and 1910 a variety of different ordnance was mounted on the battery, on which the Royal Naval Reserve carried out gun drill. The buildings inside **Fort Charlotte** have been variously used as the town jail and courthouse (1837-75), custom house, coastguard station, RNR depot and armoury, and drill hall for the Territorial Army.

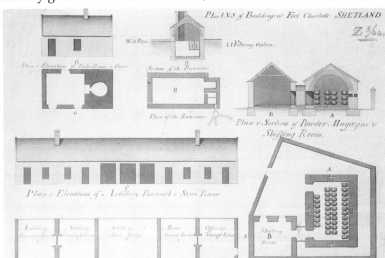

*The magazine and shifting room and other buildings as they were in 1783.*
(Reproduced by permission of the Trustees of the National Library of Scotland).

lthough the monuments in Historic Scotland's care end in date with **Fort Charlotte**, the history of Shetland continues. Many of the relatively recent remains that survive in the landscape can seem, with the advent of oil wealth and the consumer society, almost as remote from us as those of prehistoric times.

Of particular interest are the monuments of the sea: small harbours and landing places, piers and warehouses, boat-noosts (shelters at the head of beaches) and, most of all, the deserted building footings of the many haaf-fishing stations, such as Stenness and Fethaland, from which in the summer months men rowed out on the perilous business of open-boat line fishing.

Also closely linked with the sea, or at least with Shetland's position in the seas, are the well-preserved remains of military and naval presence in two World Wars. Coastal defence batteries, with guns still in position, survive on Bressay and Vementry, and elsewhere are remains of anti-aircraft installations, troop accommodation, airfields and seaplane stations.

If they survive, these more modern monuments may come to illustrate important phases of Shetland's history for future generations just as vividly as the monuments described in this booklet illustrate the past for us today.

*A naval gun installed in 1917 to guard the anchorage at Swarback's Minn.*

P D Anderson, *Robert Stewart, Earl of Orkney, Lord of Shetland, 1533-1593* (Edinburgh 1982)

P D Anderson, *Black Patie: The Life and Times of Patrick Stewart, Earl of Orkney, Lord of Shetland,* (Edinburgh 1992)

P J Ashmore, *Jarlshof: A Walk Through The Past* (Edinburgh 1993)

G Donaldson, *Shetland Life under Earl Patrick* (Edinburgh 1958)

M Finnie, *Shetland: An Illustrated Architectural Guide* (Edinburgh 1990)

N Fojut, *A Guide to Prehistoric and Viking Shetland* (Lerwick 1986)

J R C Hamilton, *Excavations at Jarlshof, Shetland* (Edinburgh 1956)

A Ritchie, *Exploring Scotland's Heritage. Orkney and Shetland* (Edinburgh 1985)

A Ritchie, *Scotland BC* (Edinburgh 1988)

A Ritchie, *Picts* (Edinburgh 1989)

A Ritchie, *Invaders of Scotland* (Edinburgh 1991)

Royal Commission on the Ancient Monuments of Scotland, *Inventory of the Ancient Monuments of Orkney and Shetland*, 3 vols (Edinburgh 1946)

B Smith (ed) *Shetland Archaeology* (Lerwick 1985)

C Tabraham, *Scottish Castles and Fortifications* (Edinburgh 1990)

The authors acknowledge the valuable help and advice of Peter Anderson and John Ballantyne in writing this guidebook.

Printed in Scotland for HMSO by C.C.No. 6033  2/93